ESSENTIALS OF ONENESS THEOLOGY

DAVID K. BERNARD

ESSENTIALS OF ONENESS THEOLOGY

ISBN 0-912315-89-X

All Scripture quotations in this book are from the King James Version of the Bible unless otherwise identified.

Printed in United States of America.

WORD AFLAME PRESS
pentecostalpublishing.com

Author's Preface

Essentials of Oneness Theology was first presented as a paper at "Aspects of the Oneness Pentecostal Movement," a symposium sponsored by Harvard Divinity School on July 5-7, 1984, in Cambridge, Massachusetts. Of the ten major papers presented at the symposium, this was the only one presented by a United Pentecostal and the only one to deal directly with the Oneness doctrine itself. The purpose of the paper was to present the essential elements of the Oneness belief, to distinguish it clearly from trinitarianism, and to answer objections trinitarians might raise.

Since many people, including trinitarians, have expressed great interest in the paper, it was prepared for publication. Only a few minor changes have been made, the most notable one being the addition of a quotation from W. A. Criswell's writings.

It is hoped that this booklet will have a twofold role: (1) a brief, convenient reference for Oneness believers and (2) a concise but thorough introduction to Oneness for those outside the movement.

For a detailed discussion of the Oneness doctrine, the reader is referred to the author's book entitled *The Oneness of God*.

David K. Bernard

Essentials of Oneness Theology

According to one estimate, a fourth of American Pentecostals adhere to the doctrine known as Oneness.[1] In church history, many have independently formulated a form of Oneness theology including, for example, the modalists and Sabellians in the ante-Nicene era, Michael Servetus (1531), John Miller (1876), Andrew Urshan (1910), R. E. McAlister, John Schaepe, and Frank Ewart (1913), and the True Jesus Church in China (1917). Consequently Oneness theology cannot be analyzed solely by the historical development of the modern Oneness movement; serious attention must be given to the biblical texts which have prompted its persistent reoccurrence within Christendom. This paper will identify the distinctive tenets of Oneness theology from the perspective of a Oneness Pentecostal, present their biblical basis, and contrast them with Trinitarianism.

The Oneness doctrine can be presented succinctly in two propositions: (1) there is one indivisible God with no distinction of persons; (2) Jesus Christ is all the fullness of the Godhead incarnate. All titles of the Deity can be applied to Him and all aspects of the divine personality are manifest in Him.

Radical Monotheism

The basis of Oneness theology is a radical concept of monotheism. Simply stated, God is absolutely and indivisibly one. There are no essential distinctions or divisions in His eternal nature. All the names and titles of the Deity, such as Elohim, Yahweh, Adonai, Father, Word, and Holy Spirit refer to one and the same being, or—in Trinitarian terminology—to one person. Any plurality associated with God is only a plurality of attributes, titles, roles, manifestations, modes of activity, or relationships to man.

This is the historic position of Judaism. Both Oneness and Jewish believers find the classic expression of this belief in Deuteronomy 6:4: "Hear, O Israel: The LORD our God is one LORD." Many other Old Testament passages, particularly in Isaiah, affirm strict monotheism and are interpreted literally to exclude any plurality in the Deity. For example: "Before me there was no God formed, neither shall there be after me. I, even I, am the LORD; and beside me there is no saviour" (Isaiah 43:10-11). "I am God, and there is none else; I am God, and there is none like me" (Isaiah 46:9).

No Old Testament passage explicitly enunciates Trinitarian doctrine; one cannot derive it from an exegesis of Old Testament texts alone. If threeness is an essential part of God's nature, He did not reveal this to His chosen people. If correct, Trinitarianism stands alone as a key aspect of God's nature totally unknown in the Old Testament but revealed in the New Testament. If God is a Trinity, then Abraham, the father of the faithful of all ages, did not comprehend the nature of the Deity he worshiped.

Oneness believers offer the following explanations for Old Testament passages that Trinitarians cite as allusions to the Trinity.

* The use of the plural word *Elohim* does not denote a plurality of persons, but is a characteristic way to express greatness or majesty in the Hebrew language.[2]

* The use of the divine plural in the phrase "Let us make man in our image" can be viewed in several ways: (1) God conversing with angels (as Jews explain); (2) God counselling with His own will (as in Ephesians 1:11); (3) a plural pronoun simply agreeing with the plural noun *Elohim;* (4) a majestic or literary plural; or (5) a prophetic reference to the future manifestation of the Son of God. Significantly, in fulfilling this verse, God created Adam as one person, with one body, mind, personality, spirit and will.

* References to the Son are prophetic of the man Christ, pointing to God's future manifestation in flesh.

* References to the Spirit of God, the Word of God, and the wisdom of God do not imply a plurality of persons any more than when one speaks of the spirit, word, or wisdom of a man.

* All Old Testament theophanies can easily be seen as manifestations of the one omnipresent, omnipotent God. While the "angel of the LORD" is apparently a theophany in many passages, occasionally the phrase

denotes a literal angel distinguished from God.

* The attribution of human body parts to God is anthropomorphic, since as a Spirit God does not have a permanent, physical body apart from the Son of Mary.

* Trinitarians often explain that the monotheistic passages used to show Oneness merely speak of perfect agreement and unity among the Trinity, excluding a plurality of false deities but not a plurality of persons in the true God. However, neither the biblical writers nor their original audiences understood this to be so. Furthermore, this view would allow outright polytheism, for many distinct deities could exist in perfect agreement and harmony.

* Trinitarians point out that the Hebrew word used to describe God's oneness is *echad*, which can mean one in agreement. However, it can also mean absolute numerical oneness and is so used many times in Scripture. It must be interpreted as such when it refers to God, or else it would not exclude polytheism as the passages in question clearly intend. To the extent that *echad* connotes a unity of plural things, it signifies the unity of God's multiple attributes.

Turning to the New Testament, Oneness exponents stress the importance of exegeting in light of context and culture. The original speakers and writers were strictly monotheistic Jews who had no thought of introducing a dramatic new revelation of plurality in the Godhead. Neither writers nor readers thought in Trinitarian categories, for both the doctrine and the terminology of the Trinity had yet to be formulated. Many New Testament passages affirm Old Testament monotheism.[3] Neither testament uses the word *Trinity* or associates the word *three* or the word *persons* with the Deity in any significant way.[4] The only passage to use the word *person* (*hypostasis*) in relation to God is Hebrews 1:3, which says the Son is the image of God's own person—literally "substance"—not a separate person or substance.

While Trinitarians concede that their doctrine of the Godhead is a mystery to finite human minds, Oneness adherents maintain that God's oneness is no mystery but is clearly revealed in Scripture to those who will believe. For them, the true mystery of the Godhead is the Incarnation (I Timothy 3:16), and that has been revealed.

In evaluating the Oneness position, it is interesting to note the conclusions of *The New Catholic Encyclopedia:* "There is the recognition on the part of exegetes and biblical theologians . . . that one should not speak of Trinitarianism in the New Testament without serious qualifications. . . . New Testament exegesis is now accepted as having shown that not only the verbal idiom but even the patterns of thought characteristic of the patristic and conciliar development would have been quite foreign to the mind and culture of the New Testament writers."[5] Similarly, Protestant theologian Emil Brunner wrote, "The doctrine of the Trinity itself, however, is not a biblical doctrine and this indeed not by accident but of necessity. It is the product of theological reflection upon the problem. . . . The ecclesiastical doctrine of the Trinity is not only the product of genuine Biblical thought, it is also the product of philosophical speculation, which is remote from the thought of the Bible."[6]

The Absolute Deity of Jesus Christ

Oneness theologians identify Jesus Christ as the incarnation of the one God, based on a literal interpretation of Colossians 2:9-10, which states, "For in him dwelleth all the fulness of the Godhead bodily. And ye are complete in him, which is the head of all principality and power." All names and titles of the Deity—such as Yahweh, Father and Holy Spirit—properly apply to Jesus. Jesus is not just the incarnation of one person of a Trinity, but the incarnation of all the character, quality and personality of the one indivisible God.

Oneness affirms in the strongest of terms that Jesus is God in the Old Testament sense, maintaining that New testament writers meant this when they called Jesus God. That is, the one and only God of the Old Testament incarnated Himself as Jesus Christ. "God was in Christ, reconciling the world unto himself" (II Corinthians 5:19). To use biblical terminology, Jesus is the image of the invisible God, God manifest in flesh, our God and Savior, and the express image of God's substance.[7]

W. A. Criswell, pastor of the First Baptist Church of Dallas, Texas, and past president of the Southern Baptist Convention, described the deity of Christ in terms identical to the Oneness position in his *Expository Sermons on Revelation.*

I often wonder at people who think that in heaven they are going to see three Gods. If you ever see three Gods, then what the Mohammedan says about you is true and what the Jewish neighbor says about you is true. You are not a monotheist, you are a polytheist. You believe in a multiplication of Gods, plural. "Hear, O Israel, the Lord thy God is one God." We know God as our Father, we know God as our Saviour and we know God by His Spirit in our hearts. But there are not three Gods. The true Christian is a monotheist. There is one

God. "I and my Father are one." "He that hath seen me hath seen the Father." The Lord God is He that speaks. It is He that John saw when he turned around. The only God you will ever see is the Lord God whom John saw in the vision of the lampstands. The only God you will ever feel is the Lord God's Spirit in your heart. The only God there is, is the great Father of us all. The one Lord God, Christ. In the Old Testament we call Him Jehovah. In the New Testament, the New Covenant, we call Him Jesus. The one great God, standing in authority and in judgment and in judicial dignity among His churches, here today, watching over us. "I saw one like [a great mystical symbol] unto the Son of man."[8]

It is the very Lord God who is coming, for Christ Jesus is God of this universe. We are not going to see three Gods in heaven. Never persuade yourself that in glory we are going to look at God No. 1 and God No. 2 and God No. 3. No! There is one great Lord God. We know Him as our Father, we know Him as our Saviour, we know Him as the Holy Spirit in our hearts. There is one God and this is the great God, called in the Old Testament, Jehovah, and, incarnate, called in the New Testament Jesus, the Prince of heaven, who is coming.[9]

Oneness applies all titles of the Deity to Jesus:
* Jesus is Yahweh of the Old Testament. This is established by studying many Old Testament statements concerning Yahweh that the New Testament applies to Jesus. For example, in Isaiah 45:23 Yahweh said, "Unto me every knee shall bow, every tongue shall swear," but in Romans 14:10-11 and Philippians 2:10-11 Paul applied this prophecy to Christ. The Old Testament describes Yahweh as the Almighty, I am, only Savior, Lord of lords, First and Last, only Creator, Holy One, Redeemer, Judge,

Shepherd and Light; yet the New Testament gives all these titles to Jesus Christ.

* Jesus is the Father. "His name shall be called . . . The mighty God, The everlasting Father" (Isaiah 9:6). "I and my Father are one" (John 10:30). "The Father is in me, and I in him" (John 10:38). "He that hath seen me hath seen the Father" (John 14:9). Jesus is the father of overcomers (Revelation 21:6-7), and He promised not to leave His disciples as fatherless (John 14:18). The Bible attributes many works both to the Father and to Jesus: resurrecting Christ's body, sending the Paraclete, drawing men to God, answering prayer, sanctifying believers, and resurrecting the dead.

* The Holy Spirit is literally the Spirit that was in Jesus Christ. "The Spirit of truth . . . dwelleth with you, and shall be in you. I will not leave you comfortless: I will come to you" (John 14:17-18). "The Lord is that Spirit" (II Corinthians 3:17). The Holy Spirit is the Spirit of the Son and the Spirit of Jesus Christ (Galatians 4:6; Philippians 1:19). The New Testament ascribes the following works both to Jesus and to the Holy Spirit: moving on prophets of old, resurrection of Christ's body, work as the Paraclete, giving words to believers in time of persecution, intercession, sanctification, and indwelling of believers. While not rejecting Trinitarianism, Lewis Smedes has acknowledged, "The experience of the Spirit is the experience with the Lord. In the new age, the Lord is the Spirit. . . . The Spirit is the ascended Jesus in His earthly action. . . . The Spirit is Christ in His redemptive functions. . . . This suggests that we do not serve a biblical purpose by insisting on the Spirit as a person who is separate from the person whose name is Jesus."[10]

Finally, Oneness teachers identify Jesus as the One on the throne in heaven, by comparing the description of Jesus in Revelation 1 with that of the One on the throne in Revelation 4 and by noting that "God and the Lamb" is one being in Revelation 22:3-4. As exemplified by Bernard Ramm, Trinitarians are ambivalent as to whether they will see one divine being or three divine beings in heaven,[11] but Oneness believers strongly reject any notion of three visible beings as tritheism.

Father, Son, and Holy Ghost

We must not suppose that Oneness denies the Father, Son, and Holy Ghost. It simply provides nontrinitarian definitions for these biblical terms. The title of Father refers to God's roles as father of all creation, father of the only begotten Son, and father of the born-again believer. The title of Son refers to God's incarnation, for the man Christ was literally conceived by the Spirit of God (Matthew 1:18-20; Luke 1:35). The title of Holy Spirit describes the fundamental character of God's nature. Holiness forms the basis of His moral attributes, while spirituality forms the basis of His nonmoral attributes. The title specifically refers to God in activity, particularly His work in anointing, regenerating, and indwelling man.

Oneness, therefore, affirms the multiple roles and works described by the terms Father, Son, and Spirit. In contrast to Trinitarianism, however, it denies that these titles reflect an essential threeness in God's nature and it affirms that all exist simultaneously in Christ. The terms can also be understood in God's revelation to man: Father refers to God in family relationship to man; Son refers to God incarnate; and Spirit refers to God in activity. For example, one man can have three significant relationships or functions—such as administrator, teacher, and counsellor—and yet be one person in every sense of the word. God is not defined by or limited to an essential threeness.

As we have already seen, the divine nature of Jesus Christ the Son of God is identified as the Father and the Holy Spirit. Moreover, the Father and the Holy Spirit are identified as one and the same being. The term Holy Spirit simply describes what the Father is. The Holy Spirit is literally the Father of Jesus, since Jesus was conceived by the Holy Spirit. The Bible calls the Holy Spirit the Spirit of Yahweh, the Spirit of God, and the Spirit of the Father. The Bible attributes many works of God the Father to the Spirit as well, such as resurrecting Christ and indwelling, comforting, sanctifying and resurrecting believers.

Oneness teachers offer the following explanations of New Testament passages often used to demonstrate the existence of a Trinity.

* Plural references to the Father and the Son simply distinguish between Christ's deity and humanity.

* Other plural references to God distinguish between various manifestations, attributes, roles, or relationships that the one God has. For example, II Corinthians 13:14 describes three aspects, attributes, or works of God— grace, love, and communion—and links them with names or titles that correspond most directly with these qualities—Lord Jesus Christ, God, and Holy Ghost. Likewise, I Peter 1:2 mentions the foreknowledge of God the Father, the sanctification of the Spirit, and the blood of Jesus.

* The baptism of Christ was not meant to introduce to the devout Jewish onlookers a radical, innovative

doctrine of plurality in the Godhead, but signified the authoritative anointing of Jesus as the Messiah. A correct understanding of God's omnipresence dispels any notion that the heavenly voice and dove require separate persons.

* Christ's description of the Holy Ghost as "another Comforter" in John 14 indicates a difference of form or relationship, i.e., Christ in Spirit rather than in flesh.

* John 17 speaks of the unity of the man Christ with the Father. As a man Christ was one with God in mind, purpose and will, and we can be one with God in this sense. However, other passages teach that Christ is one with God in a sense that we cannot be, in that He is God Himself.

* Saying Jesus is at the right hand of God does not denote a physical positioning of two beings with two bodies, for God is a Spirit and does not have a physical body outside of Jesus Christ. This view would be indistinguishable from ditheism. Rather, the phrase is an idiomatic expression from the Old Testament, denoting that Christ possesses all the power, authority, and preeminence of God.[12]

* Paul's epistles typically include a salutation such as: "Grace to you and peace from God our Father, and the Lord Jesus Christ" (Romans 1:7). This emphasizes the need to acknowledge not only God's role as Father and Creator, but also God's revelation in flesh as Jesus Christ. The Greek conjunction *kai* can mean "even," thus identifying the Father and Jesus as the same being. In similar passages, such as II Thessalonians 1:12 and Titus 2:13, Granville Sharp's rule applies: If two personal nouns of the same gender, number, and case are con-

nected by *kai,* if the first has the definite article and the second does not, they both relate to the same person.

* "The God and Father of our Lord Jesus Christ" denotes a covenant relationship much as "the God of Abraham." It serves to remind us of the promises Christ won as a sinless man, which are available from "the God of Jesus Christ" to those who have faith in Christ.

* The *kenosis* of Christ described in Philippians 2:6-8 does not mean Christ emptied Himself of attributes of deity such as omnipresence, omniscience, and omnipotence, for then Christ would be merely a demigod. The Spirit of Christ retained all attributes of deity even while He manifested all of His character in flesh. This passage only refers to the limitations Christ imposed on Himself relative to His human life. The *kenosis* was a voluntary surrender of glory, dignity, and godly prerogatives, not an abdication of His nature of deity. The union of deity and humanity that was Jesus Christ was equal with God and proceeded from God, but became humble and obedient unto death.

* The vision of the One on the throne and the Lamb in Revelation 5 is symbolic only. The One on the throne represents all the Deity, while the Lamb represents the Son in His human, sacrificial role.

The Son

As we have seen, Oneness exponents define the term *Son* to mean the manifestation of the one God in flesh. They maintain that *Son* can refer to the human nature of Christ alone (as in "the Son died") or to the union of deity and humanity (as in "the Son shall return to earth in glory"). However, they insist that the term can never be used apart from God's incarnation; it can never refer to deity alone. They reject the nonbiblical term "God the Son," the doctrine of the eternal Son, and the doctrine of the eternal begetting.[13] The phrase "only begotten Son" does not refer to an inexplicable, spiritual generation of the Son from the Father, but to the miraculous conception of Jesus in the virgin's womb by the Holy Spirit.

In establishing the beginning of the Son, Oneness believers appeal to these scriptural passages: "The Holy Ghost shall come upon thee, and the power of the Highest shall overshadow thee: therefore also that holy thing which shall be born of thee shall be called the Son of God" (Luke 1:35). "But when the fulness of the time was come, God sent forth his Son, made of a woman, made under the law" (Galatians 4:4). "Thou art my Son, this day have I begotten thee" (Hebrews 1:5). They point to a time when the distinctive role of the Son will end, when the redemptive purpose for which God manifested Himself in flesh will no longer exist. This does not imply that Christ's immortal, glorified human body will cease to exist, but only that the mediatorial work and reign of the Son will end. The role of the Son will be submerged back into the greatness of God, who will remain in His original role as Father, Creator, and Ruler of all. "Then shall the Son also himself be subject unto him that put all things under him, that God may be all in all" (I Corinthians 15:28).

Oneness believers emphasize the two natures in Christ, using this fact to explain the plural references to Father and Son in the Gospels. As Father, Jesus sometimes acted and spoke from His divine self-consciousness; as Son He sometimes acted and spoke from His human self-consciousness.[14] The two natures never acted in conflict, for they were united into one person.

Aside from their emphasis on the two natures of Christ, Oneness teachers have given inadequate attention to many areas of Christology. Some have made statements that sound Apollinarian because of failure to define and use terms precisely, but Oneness scholars overwhelmingly reject this implication. If carefully developed, Oneness may be seen as compatible with the Christological formulation of the Council of Chalcedon, namely that Christ has two complete natures—deity and humanity—but is only one person. However, Oneness believers do not rely on the creeds to formulate doctrinal positions, but look solely to the Scriptures, which reveal the complete deity of Christ, the complete humanity of Christ, and the essential and total union of deity and humanity in the Incarnation.

In a few cases, Oneness believers have taken Christological positions not only inconsistent with Chalcedon but with their own position of Oneness. For example, some have explained Christ's cry on the cross, "My God, my God, why hast thou forsaken me?" as signifying that the Spirit of God departed from Jesus at that moment. Not only does this view destroy the unity of Christ's person, but it also undercuts the belief in His absolute deity. It is more consistent to view this as signifying the punishment Christ suffered as He took on the sins of the world. He actually tasted death for every man; He felt the utter separation from God that a sinner will feel in eternity.

Within Oneness circles there are also different views expressed on the peccability of Christ. A consistent application of Oneness principles would indicate that Christ was impeccable. Occasionally, someone will imply that Jesus became fully aware of His deity or became fully divine only at some point in His adult life, such as at His baptism. This position is inconsistent with the Oneness doctrines of the begotten Son and the absolute deity of Christ, and is strongly rejected by the movement.

Oneness teachers offer the following explanations for questions raised with respect to their doctrine of the Son.

* According to Hebrews 1:2, God made the worlds by the Son. Certainly, the Spirit (God) who was in the Son was also the Creator of the worlds. This passage may also indicate that God predicated the entire work of creation upon the future manifestation of the Son. God foreknew that man would sin, but He also foreknew that through the Son man could be saved and could fulfill God's original purpose in creation. As John Miller stated, "Though He did not pick up His humanity till the fulness of time, yet He used it, and acted upon it, from all eternity."[15]

* Hebrews 1:6 calls the Son the firstbegotten or the firstborn. An Arian interpretation of this verse would say that God created a divine Son before He created anything else, but this is inconsistent with Oneness theology, and the movement strongly rejects any form of Arianism. The Son is the firstborn in the sense of the humanity: (1) He is the first and only begotten Son in that He was conceived by the Spirit; (2) the Incarnation existed in God's mind from the beginning and formed the basis for all subsequent actions; (3) as a man, Jesus is the first to conquer sin and so is the firstborn of the spiritual family of God; (4) as a man, Jesus is the first to conquer death and so is the firstborn of the resurrection; (5) just as the firstborn son has the position of preeminence, so Jesus is the head of all creation and of the church.

* Jesus preexisted the Incarnation, not as the eternal Son but as the eternal Spirit of God. The Son was sent from the Father, but this terminology simply indicates that the Father enacted His preexisting plan at a certain point in time and that the Son was divinely appointed to accomplish a certain task. In the same way, John the Baptist was a man sent from God, but he did not preexist his arrival into this world.

* The prayers of Christ represent the struggle of the human will as it submitted to the divine will. They represent Jesus praying from His human self-consciousness not from His divine, for by definition God does not need to pray. This line of reasoning also explains other examples of the inferiority of the Son in power and knowledge. If these examples demonstrate a plurality of persons, they establish the subordination of one person to the other, contrary to the Trinitarian doctrine of coequality.

* Other examples of communication, conversation, or expression of love between Father and Son are explained as communication between the eternal God and the man Christ. If used to demonstrate a distinction of persons, they would establish separate centers of consciousness in the Godhead, which is in effect polytheism.

The Logos

The Logos (Word) of John 1 is not equivalent to the title *Son* in Oneness theology as it is in Trinitarianism. *Son* is limited to the Incarnation, but *Logos* is not. The Logos is God's self expression, "God's means of self disclosure," or "God uttering Himself."[16] Before the Incarnation, the Logos was the unexpressed thought, plan, and mind of God, which had a reality no human thought can have because of God's perfect foreknowledge and, in the case of the Incarnation, God's predestination. In the beginning, the Logos was with God, not as a separate person but as God Himself—pertaining to and belonging to God much like a man and his word. In the fullness of time God put flesh on the Logos; He expressed Himself in flesh.

Theology of the Name

Oneness places strong emphasis on the doctrine of the name of God as expressed in both Old and New Testaments. For people in biblical times, "the name is a part of the person, an extension of the personality of the individual."[17] Specifically, the name of God represents the revelation of His presence, character, power, and authority. In the Old Testament, Yahweh was the redemptive name of God and the unique name by which He distinguished Himself from false gods. In the New Testament, however, Oneness teachers maintain that God accompanied the revelation of Himself in flesh with a new name. That name is Jesus, which includes and supersedes Yahweh, since it literally means Yahweh-Savior or Yahweh is Salvation. Although others have borne the name Jesus, the Lord Jesus Christ is the only one who is actually what that name describes.

While Trinitarians see the name Jesus as the human name of God the Son, Oneness adherents see it as the redemptive name of God in the New Testament, which carries with it the power and authority needed by the church.[18] They appeal to these passages of Scripture: "If ye shall ask any thing in my name, I will do it" (John 14:14). "Neither is there salvation in any other: for there is none other name under heaven given among men, whereby we must be saved" (Acts 4:12). "Through his name whosoever believeth in him shall receive remission of sins" (Acts 10:43). "Wherefore God also hath highly exalted him, and given him a name which is above every name: that at the name of Jesus every knee should bow, of things in heaven, and things in earth, and things under the earth" (Philippians 2:9-10). "Whatsoever ye do in word or deed, do all in the name of the Lord Jesus" (Colossians 3:17).

They note that the early church prayed, preached, taught, healed the sick, performed miracles, cast out unclean spirits, and baptized in the name of Jesus. The name of Jesus is not meant as a magical formula; it is effective only through faith in Jesus and a relationship with Him. Nevertheless, the Christian should actually use the spoken name Jesus in prayer and baptism as an outward expression of faith in Jesus and in obedience to God's Word.

Formula for Water Baptism

The theology of the Name and the rejection of Trinitarianism require that a Christological baptismal formula be used. The Oneness movement teaches that water baptism should be administered with the invocation of the name Jesus. Usually, the titles of Lord or Christ are used as an added identification, as in the Book of Acts. Exponents of Oneness point out that every time the Bible describes the formula used at an actual baptism, it always describes the name Jesus (Acts 2:38; 8:16; 10:48; 19:5; 22:16). In addition to these historical accounts in Acts, the epistles use many allusions to the Jesus Name formula (Romans 6:4; I Corinthians 1:13; 6:11; Galatians 3:27;

Colossians 2:12).

Matthew 28:19 is given special attention, because it is the only biblical passage that could possibly be an allusion to any other formula. It is explained as follows.

* The grammar of the verse denotes a singular name. Since Jesus is at once Father, Son, and Spirit, since He came in His Father's name and will send the Spirit in His name, the one name of Matthew 28:19 must be Jesus. Many Trinitarians recognize that the name is singular and identify it as Yahweh.[19] Oneness adherents add that God's salvific name in the New Testament is not Yahweh but Jesus.

* The context demands a Christological formula. Christ said, in effect, "I have all power, so go and make disciples unto me, baptizing them in my name." Again, many Trinitarian scholars have recognized the force of this argument.[20] Consequently they argue that this verse does not record the *ipsissima verba* (very words) of Jesus but a paraphrase by Matthew or even a later liturgical change by copyists. Significantly, Eusebius often quoted this verse before the Council of Nicea as "in my name." Other Trinitarians propose that the church did not originally see this verse as an actual baptismal formula. For Oneness believers the accepted wording of Matthew 28:19 does not pose a textual problem; they see the existing words as a description of the Jesus Name formula.

* The parallel accounts of the great commission in Mark 16 and Luke 24 both describe the name of Jesus.

* The early church, which included Matthew, carried out Christ's instructions by baptizing in the name of Jesus.

While church historians generally agree that the

original baptismal formula was indeed "in the name of Jesus," not all Trinitarians agree that this biblical phrase denotes the oral invocation of the name Jesus. Oneness teachers affirm that it does because:

* This is the most natural, literal reading.

* In Acts 22:16 Ananias told Paul to invoke the name of the Lord at baptism.

* Acts 15:17 and James 2:7 indicate that the name of Jesus was invoked over Christians at a specific point in time. In the latter verse, *The Amplified Bible* even identifies this as water baptism.

* When the disciples prayed, laid hands on the sick, and cast out devils "in the name of Jesus," they always invoked the name orally (Acts 3:6; 16:18; 19:13).

* The phrase does signify the power and authority of Jesus, but the power and authority represented by a name is always invoked by actually using the proper name.

* If this phrase does not describe a baptismal formula, then neither does Matthew 28:19, since the grammatical construction is identical. However, this would leave the church without any means to distinguish Christian baptism from pagan baptisms, Jewish proselyte baptism, and John's baptism.

* Although the precise wording of the baptismal accounts differs, all (including Matthew 28:19) describe the same name: Jesus.

Receiving the Holy Spirit
Trinitarian Pentecostals have often been accused of glorifying the Holy Spirit at the expense of the Son, and they sharply distinguish between receiving Christ and receiving the Holy Spirit. The Oneness doctrine avoids

this problem. To receive Christ is to receive the Holy Spirit, and vice versa.

Oneness Pentecostals typically expect the baptism of the Holy Spirit to follow immediately upon repentance, as part of an apostolic conversion experience. The disciples waited until Pentecost for their Spirit baptism only because it was not available prior to the founding of the New Testament church. Cornelius and his household immediately received the Spirit when they believed the preaching of Peter. Paul was filled with the Holy Spirit as part of his three-day conversion experience. The Samaritans in Acts 8 and the disciples of John the Baptist in Acts 19 received the Holy Spirit when they came into a fullness of faith in Christ.

Unlike other Pentecostals, then, Oneness Pentecostals see the baptism of the Holy Spirit as an integral part of receiving Christ. For them it is not a new encounter with another member of the Trinity, nor a second or third "work of grace," but part of new life in Christ.

Conclusion

In contradistinction to Trinitarianism, Oneness asserts that: (1) God is indivisibly one in number with no distinction of persons; (2) God's oneness is no mystery; (3) Jesus is the absolute fullness of the Godhead; He is at once Elohim, Yahweh, Father, Son, and Holy Spirit; (4) the Son of God was begotten after the flesh and did not exist from eternity past—the term only refers to God's incarnation in Christ; (5) the Logos (Word) is not a separate person, but the mind, thought, plan, activity, or expression of the Father; (6) Jesus is the revealed name of God in the New Testament, and represents salvation, power and authority from God; (7) water baptism should be administered by orally invoking the name Jesus as part of the baptismal formula; and (8) believers will definitely see only one divine being in heaven: Jesus Christ.

The Oneness doctrine does not destroy any doctrine essential to Christianity, from the sole authority of Scripture to the substitutionary atonement to justification by faith. In fact, Oneness believers affirm that their doctrine upholds biblical Christianity in at least three specific ways: (1) it restores biblical terminology and biblical patterns of thought on the subject of the Godhead, clearly establishing New Testament Christianity as the spiritual heir of Old Testament Judaism; (2) it upholds the absolute deity of Jesus Christ, revealing His true identity; (3) it places biblical emphasis on the name of Jesus, making the power of His name available to the believer. In short, to them the Oneness doctrine is a crucial element in restoring biblical beliefs and apostolic power.

Footnotes

[1]Tim Dowley, et. al., eds. *Eerdmans' Handbook to the History of the Church* (Grand Rapids: Eerdmans, 1977), p. 619.

[2]"The Hebrews pluralized nouns to express greatness or majesty."

[3]Henry Flanders and Bruce Cresson, *Introduction to the Bible* (New York: John Wiley & Sons, 1973), p. 48 n. 8.

[3]Mark 12:29-30; Romans 3:30; I Corinthians 8:4; Galatians 3:20; Ephesians 4:6; I Timothy 2:5; James 2:19; Revelation 4:2.

[4]Scholars agree that I John 5:7 was not part of the original text. Even if genuine, it does not divide Father, Word, and Spirit into separate persons any more than a man, his word, and his spirit are separate persons. It concludes, "These three are one."

[5]"Trinity, Holy," *The New Catholic Encyclopedia* (New York: McGraw Hill, 1967), XIV, 295-305.

[6]Emil Brunner, *The Christian Doctrine of God* (Philadelphia: Westminster Press, 1949), pp. 236-39.

[7]II Corinthians 4:4; Colossians 1:15; I Timothy 3:16; Titus 2:13; Hebrews 1:3; II Peter 1:1.

[8]W. A. Criswell, *Expository Sermons on Revelation* (Grand Rapids: Zondervan, 1961-66), I, 145-46.

[9]Ibid., V, 42.

[10]Lewis Smedes, *Union with Christ*, rev. ed. (Grand Rapids: Eerdmans, 1983), pp. 41-54.

[11]Bernard Ramm, *Protestant Biblical Interpretation*, 3rd ed. (Grand Rapids: Baker, 1965), p. 171.

[12]God's right hand signifies His almightiness and sitting at God's right hand signifies preeminence. Ramm, p. 100.

[13]Trinitarians who have rejected the terminology "eternal Son" include Adam Clarke, cult expert Walter Martin, and Pentecostal Bible annotater Finis Dake. See Adam Clarke, *Clarke's Commentary* (Nashville: Abingdon, 1810), V, 360-61; Walter Martin, *The Kingdom of the Cults* (Minneapolis: Bethany House Publishers, 1965), pp. 102-03; Finis Dake, *Dake's Annotated Reference Bible* (Lawrenceville, Ga.: Dake's Bible Sales, 1963), NT, p. 139.

[14]For a Trinitarian statement of the same position, see Henry Thiessen, *Lectures in Systematic Theology*, rev ed. (Grand Rapids: Eerdmans, 1979), p. 223.

[15]John Miller, *Is God a Trinity?* 3rd ed. (Princeton, N.J.: Privately printed, 1922), pp. 96-97.

[16]Flanders and Cresson, p. 511; Miller, p. 85.

[17]Flanders and Cresson, p. 61.

[18]For a Trinitarian who advocates a similar theology of the name Jesus, see Essex Kenyon, *The Wonderful Name of Jesus* (Los Angeles: West Coast Publishing Co., 1927).

[19]James Buswell, Jr., *A Systematic Theology of the Christian Religion* (Grand Rapids: Zondervan, 1980), I, 23.

[20]See G. R. Beasley-Murray, *Baptism in the New Testament* (Grand Rapids: Eerdmans, 1962), pp. 81-84.

Works by David K. Bernard:

Pentecostal Theology Series
Vol. 1: The Oneness of God*
Vol. 2: The New Birth*
Vol. 3: In Search of Holiness (with Loretta Bernard)*
Vol. 4: Practical Holiness
A Study Guide for The Oneness of God
A Study Guide for The New Birth
A Study Guide for In Search of Holiness
A Study Guide for Practical Holiness
    (Each volume can be purchased in hardback with Study Guide included)

Biblical Theology (Other)
A Handbook of Basic Doctrines*
Doctrines of the Bible (ed. with J. L. Hall)
In the Name of Jesus
Justification and the Holy Spirit
On Being Pentecostal (with Robin Johnston)
The Oneness View of Jesus Christ
Spiritual Gifts*
God's Infallible Word
Understanding God's Word

Practical Theology
The Apostolic Church in the Twenty-first Century
The Apostolic Life
Growing a Church
The Pentecostal Minister (ed. with J. L. Hall)

Commentaries
The Message of Colossians and Philemon
The Message of Romans

Booklets
Essential Doctrines of the Bible*
Essentials of Oneness Theology
Essentials of the New Birth*
Essentials of Holiness
Understanding the Articles of Faith
Bible Doctrines and Study Guide

Church History
A History of Christian Doctrine, Vol. 1: The Post-Apostolic Age to the Middle Ages
A History of Christian Doctrine, Vol. 2: The Reformation to the Holiness Movement
A History of Christian Doctrine, Vol. 3: The Twentieth Century
Oneness and Trinity, AD 100-300
The Trinitarian Controversy in the Fourth Century

CD-ROM
Pentecostal Digital Library, Vol. 1: Complete Works by David K. Bernard
Preaching the Apostolic Faith
Teaching the Apostolic Faith
Pentecostal Pulpit Series, Vol. 3: David K. Bernard (with audiovisual CD)
An Introduction to Apostolic Pentecostal Theology (4 books)

*Available in Spanish

www.pentecostalpublishing.com